FLEXIBLY CHALLENGED MIND:
AN AUTISTIC FLOW

WRITTEN BY:
CHERICE TYRHONDA PEAGLER

ILLUSTRATIONS INSIDE BY:
TWON SMITH

Today was a tough day for Michael in his classroom setting...

Smash! Michael's hand came down on Jessie's clay model. "Why did you do that, Michael?" Ms. Peak asked. "I am angry!" "Why are you angry?" Ms. Peak tried to understand. "I don't know!" Michael yelled.

Jessie asked, "Why are you yelling, Michael?" "I don't know!" Michael explained. "Stop asking me questions!" Michael firmly suggested before poking out his tongue and hitting Jessie because Jessie was talking to him.

Ms. Peak and the assistant teacher, Ms. Bowen, looked at one another in confusion. They wanted to help Michael, but the more they talked, the more Michael said, "shut up!"

Is Michael speaking kindly? No.

What can Michael do to help him to calm his body?

* Deep breathing
* Rub his hands together
* Rub his legs
* Talk about what is bothering him
* Stress ball

* Do not speak until he is ready to speak in a controlled indoor voice
* Take a time out
* Cuddle with a favorite stuffed animal
* Get help with a difficult task
* Words of affirmation spoken to self or by someone else
* Switch activity or switch environment

* Listen to soft music
* Go to a quiet area for a break
* During a break, apply a weighted blanket
* Choose a safe and healthy hobby of interest that is known to calm self
* Ask a teacher to dim the lights to be sure the lights are not overly stimulating

Michael is having a hard time controlling his actions and words. Ms. Peak reminded Michael of the expectations in the classroom. She gave one expectation at a time to not overwhelm Michael. She explained, "We are to respect our friend's property."

What are reasons why it is a good idea to respect the property of others?

* It is not ours.
* Hard work was put into the project.
* The person could be proud of their work.
* You could cause someone to be sad.
* You would not want anyone else destroying your hard work.
* It would also be helpful to Michael if he had a conversation about how he would feel if someone destroyed his work that he cared about and worked hard to build.

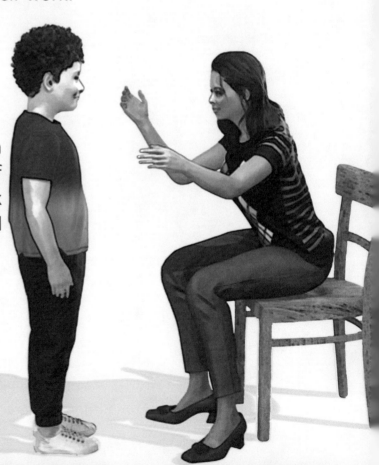

Ms. Peak also reminded Michael of his consequences.

* Not being able to interact with his friends.
* Missing out on fun activities planned in the future.
* Others not wanting to be around him.

Michael wanted to know after calming down, "What could I have done because I was mad?" He was reminded by Ms. Peak, "When you become angry there are some rules to follow: do not hurt yourself, do not hurt others, and do not destroy property. It is also important not to hurt others with words, body parts, or objects. I am proud of you that you did not hurt anyone physically, but you did destroy property that did not belong to you." Ms. Peak asked, "What do you think should happen because of your actions? If you are not able to come up with a consequence that I can agree with, I will help you with your consequence." Michael said, "I can go to the calm down area away from others for 5 minutes." Ms. Peak agreed that Michael had come up with a good consequence. Then Michael decided to say, "Sorry Jessie for smashing your model" as he walked to the calm down area.

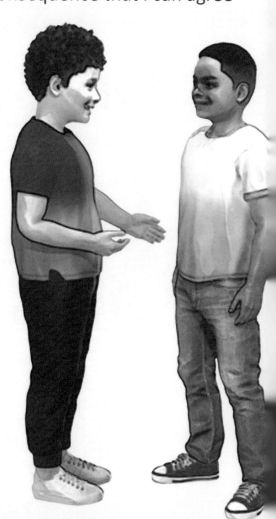

During Michael's calm down time, Ms. Peak was able to attend to the rest of the class while Ms. Bowen went over to check on Michael and talk to him more about positive decision making.

Michael was ready to listen now because he was calm and only one person was speaking to him at a time.

Ms. Bowen reminded Michael to remember his anger rules, ways to calm down, consequences, and how it can be rewarding to make positive choices.

Then Ms. Bowen asked, "What happened before you got angry Michael?" Michael said, "Olivia was taking my red crayon home." What had actually happened was that Olivia had put Michael's red crayon on his desk because she saw that it had dropped to the floor. What Michael thought was happening before his meltdown was not accurate. Ms. Bowen suggested to Michael, "Michael, before you decide to get angry, ask yourself what is making you angry and then ask for help to be sure you are getting the correct information. We have to be sure our perspective makes sense before we react."

Perspective guides our thoughts, feelings, and emotions whether accurate or not. Be mindful that one's take on a situation can be different from another person's, even after viewing the same situation. Remember to gather all information, evaluate the information, and then think of a reasonable solution. This process can take 10 seconds, 10 minutes, or longer than an hour depending on the situation. Understand that responding to a situation is different than being reactive. Understand the situation, understand yourself, and act wisely.

"Flexibly Challenged Mind: An Autistic Flow" is dedicated to any parent, caregiver, and teacher who cares for a child with autistic characteristics. The story is also for the child who has an autistic diagnosis. There are different spectrums of autism. Each spectrum brings a different challenge whether the challenge is behavioral, emotional, and/or nonverbal. Seeking resources that meet each child's needs can be challenging and time consuming. The desire to meet the child's needs can sometimes be heavy on the heart. One may sometimes feel baffled about what to do next to serve a child with autistic characteristics. Taking care of a child with autistic characteristics will affect each parent, caregiver, or teacher differently. There is a challenge presented because one must learn the child to decide the child's needs. Whatever challenge that appears, anyone guiding the autistic brain will notice that giving grace for each new day will renew one's spirit and energy to show up the next day to be a guiding light.

- Cherice TyRhonda Peagler

Please take this book to future trainings to continue to record new things that you discover about the autistic mind. Continue to communicate your thoughts to one another to help continue to increase autism awareness.

NOTES

NOTES

NOTES

NOTES

NOTES

NOTES

Printed in the USA
CPSIA information can be obtained
at www.ICGtesting.com
LVRC091605230524
781050LV00014B/23